Dinosaurs by Design

I0886609

HORNED DINOSAURS

RANKING THEIR SPEED, STRENGTH, AND SMARTS

MARK WEAKLAND

BLACK RABBIT BOOKS

Bolt is published by Black Rabbit Books
P.O. Box 3263, Mankato, Minnesota, 56002.
www.blackrabbitbooks.com
Copyright © 2020 Black Rabbit Books

Jennifer Besel, editor; Catherine Cates, interior designer; Grant Gould, cover designer; Omay Ayres, photo researcher

All rights reserved. No part of this book may be reproduced, stored in a retrieval system or transmitted in any form or by any means, electronic, mechanical, photocopying, recording, or otherwise, without written permission from the publisher.

Library of Congress Cataloging-in-Publication Data
Names: Weakland, Mark, author.
Title: Horned dinosaurs : ranking their speed, strength, and smarts / by Mark Weakland.
Description: Mankato, Minnesota : Black Rabbit Books, [2020] | Series: Bolt. Dinosaurs by design | Audience: Ages 8-12. | Audience: Grades 4 to 6. | Includes bibliographical references and index.
Identifiers: LCCN 2018011683 (print) | LCCN 2018017057 (ebook) | ISBN 9781680728309 (e-book) | ISBN 9781680728248 (library binding) | ISBN 9781644660294 (paperback)
Subjects: LCSH: Ceratopsidae—Juvenile literature.
Classification: LCC QE862.O65 (ebook) | LCC QE862.O65 W4344 2020 (print) | DDC 567.915—dc23
LC record available at https://lccn.loc.gov/2018011683

Printed in the United States. 1/19

Image Credits

Alamy: Frederick Matzen, 20–21; Stocktrek Images, Inc., 11, 15 (t); Palaeocritti.com/commons.wikimedia.org: NobuTamura, 15 (br); Science Source: Kurt Miller/Stocktrek Images, 24; Mark Hallett Paleoart, 4–5; Mohamad Haghani, 23; Walter Myers, Cover; Shutterstock: 90miles, 17, 22 (prints); Anton_Ivanov, 32; Catmando, 12 (Diabloceratops), 29 (Styracosaurus & Torosaurus); DM7, 1, 16–17 (dino); Eric Isselee, 15 (bm); ExpressionImage, 12–13 (T. rex); Herschel Hoffmeyer, 6–7, 12 (bkgd), 16 (bkgd), 29 (Triceratops), 31; Michael Rosskothen, 3, 26–27 (left dinos), 27 (r); Vlad Klok, 15 (bl); Vorobiov Oleksii 8, 8–9; Superstock: Stocktrek Images, Inc., 18–19 Every effort has been made to contact copyright holders for material reproduced in this book. Any omissions will be rectified in subsequent printings if notice is given to the publisher.

CONTENTS

CHAPTER 1

Horns, Frills, and POWER

There's a rumbling and crashing in the forest. Two horned dinosaurs are battling. Their long horns crack as they crash together.

Horned dinosaurs didn't have huge claws or sharp teeth. But they were big and strong. Their horns and **frills** protected them from **predators** and other horned dinosaurs.

Big Plant Eaters

Horned dinosaurs lived about 100 to 65 million years ago. Some were the size of cows. Others were as big as elephants. Like cows and elephants, they ate plants.

Scientists have found many horned dinosaur **fossils**. Most of their fossils have been found in North America. But some have been found in Europe and Asia.

WHERE SOME HORNED DINOSAUR FOSSILS HAVE BEEN FOUND

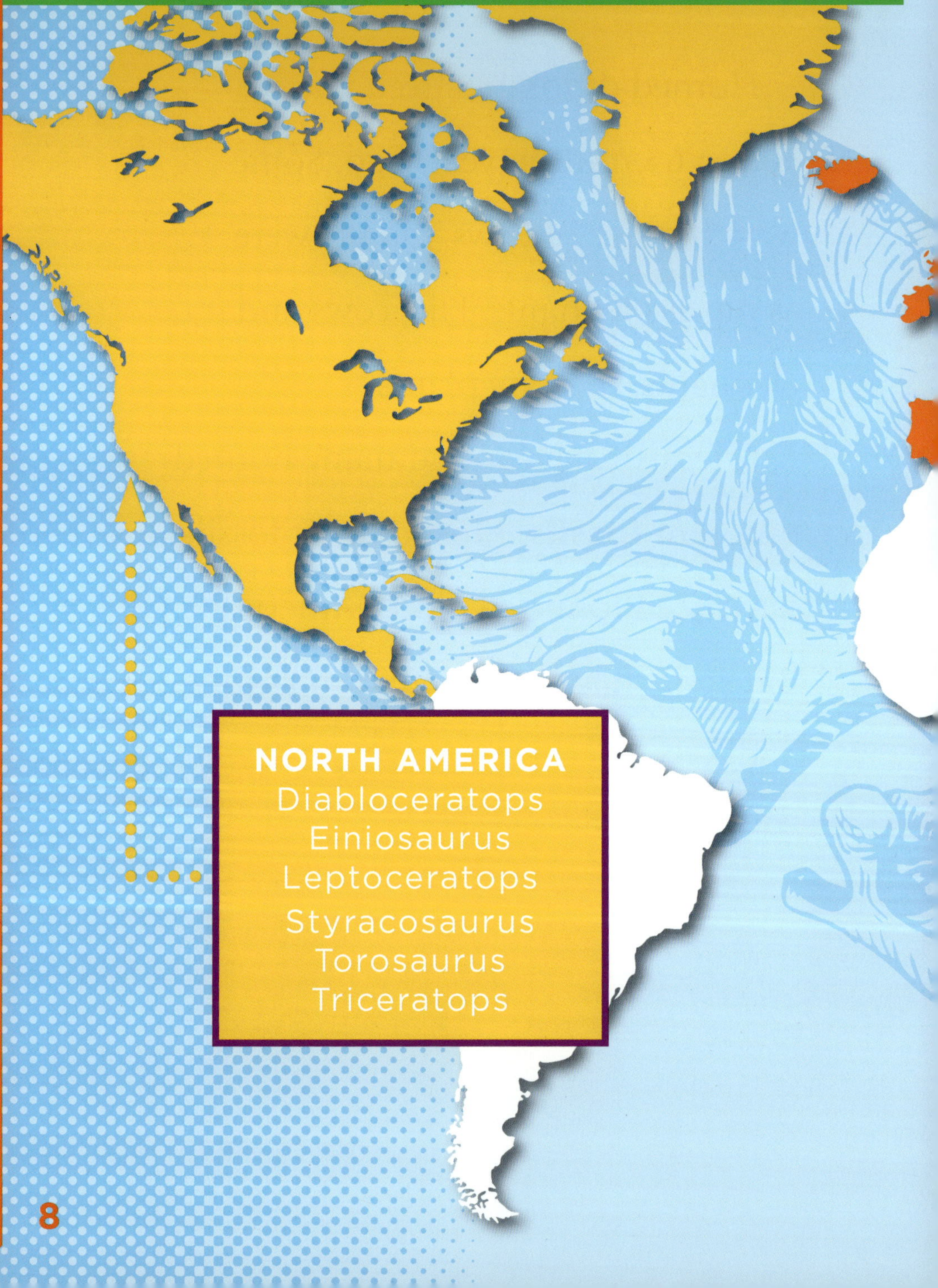

EUROPE
Ajkaceratops

CHAPTER 2

Compare the DINOS

Torosaurus

(tor-oh-SOR-us)

Torosaurus was a powerful animal. It could fight off large meat eaters. It was bigger than an elephant. Its frill was huge. And its thick legs helped it stay on its feet when attacked.

FEATURE FACTS

LENGTH	up to 25 FEET (8 METERS)
WEIGHT	up to 18,000 POUNDS (8,165 KILOGRAMS)
NUMBER OF FACE HORNS	3

Diabloceratops

(dee-AB-low-SEH-rah-tops)

Diabloceratops would have been scary to see. It had two large horns above its eyes. It also had two spikes that rose from its neck frill. The spikes and frill made this dino look **fierce**. A hungry meat eater would take one look and say, "No, thanks."

FEATURE FACTS

WEIGHT
2,000 to 4,000 pounds (907 to 1,814 kg)

LENGTH
about 18 feet (5 m)

NUMBER OF FACE HORNS
2

Ajkaceratops

(EYE-kah-SEH-rah-tops)

This little dinosaur didn't have any big horns. But it is still part of the horned dinosaur family. It had a hard "beak." All horned dinosaurs had this type of mouth.

COMPARING AVERAGE WEIGHTS

FEATURE FACTS

LENGTH about 3 FEET (1 M)

WEIGHT 30 to 40 POUNDS (14 to 18 KG)

NUMBER OF FACE HORNS 0

BULLDOG	RED FOX	AJKACERATOPS

40 to 50 POUNDS (18 to 23 kg)	6.5 to 24 POUNDS (3 to 11 kg)	30 to 40 POUNDS (14 to 18 kg)

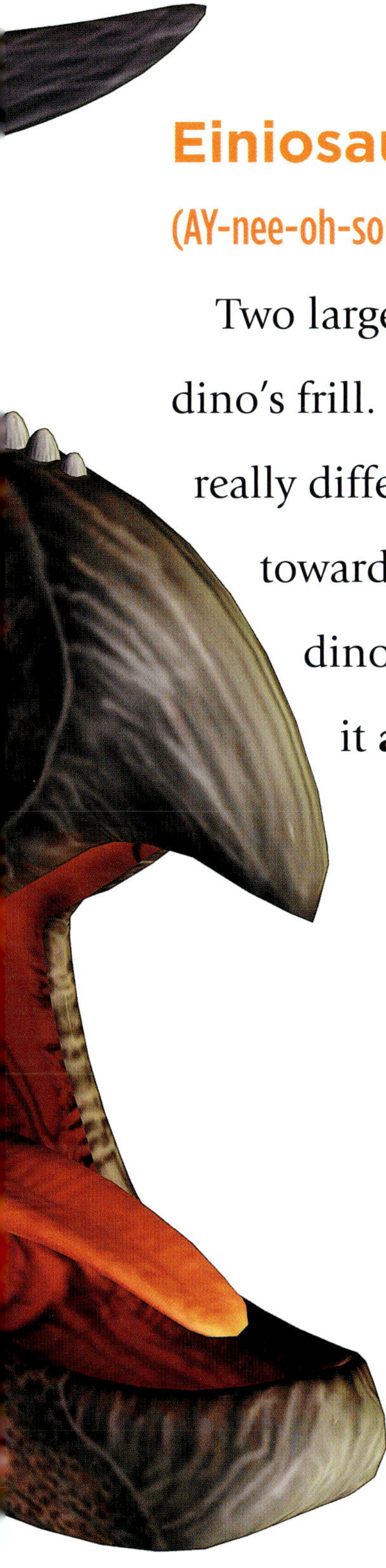

Einiosaurus

(AY-nee-oh-sor-us)

Two large spikes rose from this dino's frill. But its **snout** horn was really different. Its horn curved toward the ground. Perhaps this dinosaur used it to fight. Maybe it **attracted** females.

FEATURE FACTS

WEIGHT
2,000 to 3,000 pounds
(907 to 1,361 kg)

LENGTH
about 20 feet
(6 m)

NUMBER OF FACE HORNS
1

Triceratops

(tri-SEH-rah-tops)

Triceratops is probably the most famous horned dinosaur. Its name means "three-horned face." Its horns were long. Its legs were powerful. Its frill was made of thick bone. If Tyrannosaurus rex attacked, Triceratops was ready.

FEATURE FACTS

WEIGHT	LENGTH	NUMBER OF FACE HORNS
11,000 to 15,750 pounds (4,990 to 7,144 kg)	up to 30 feet (9 m)	3

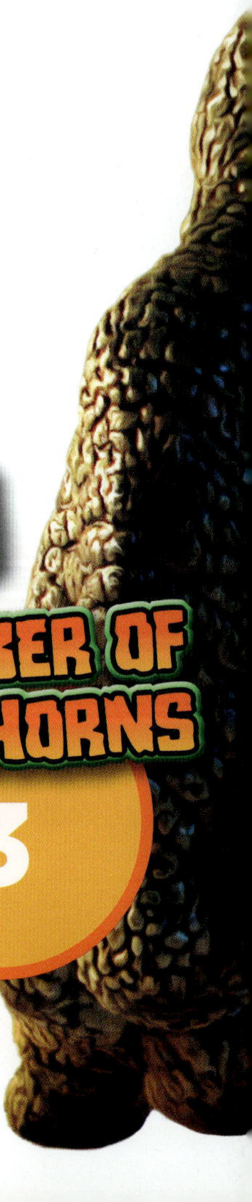

TRICERATOPS FEATURES

HORNS
FRILL
BEAK

Leptoceratops

(lep-to-SEH-rah-tops)

Leptoceratops was a smaller horned dinosaur. Its front legs were shorter than its back legs. Some scientists think this dino could walk on its hind legs. Maybe it could run away from predators.

FEATURE FACTS

WEIGHT
up to 200 pounds (91 kg)

LENGTH
6 to 9 feet (2 to 3 m)

NUMBER OF FACE HORNS
0

Horned dinosaurs usually moved slowly. But they could put on bursts of speed. Scientists think some could run as fast as a rhino. A rhino's top speed is up to 40 miles (64 kilometers) per hour

Its frill might have turned red to attract a mate.

Styracosaurus

(STY-rah-co-sor-us)

Styracosaurus was one spiky dinosaur. Six main spikes sprouted from the top of its frill. Smaller spikes pushed out from the sides. The spikes might have helped males attract females.

It also had a wicked horn on its snout. The horn might have been used for fighting. Some scientists think the males fought to **mate** with females.

FEATURE FACTS

LENGTH about 18 FEET (5 M)

WEIGHT about 6,000 POUNDS (2,722 KG)

NUMBER OF FACE HORNS 1

CHAPTER 3

Long Live the DINOSAURS

Horned dinosaurs moved slowly much of the time. But they were large and powerful. Their frills and horns helped them **survive**. And survive they did. Horned dinosaurs roamed Earth for millions of years.

COMPARE THEM!

Rank the dinos in this book. Then go find information on other horned dinos. How do they compare?

LENGTH

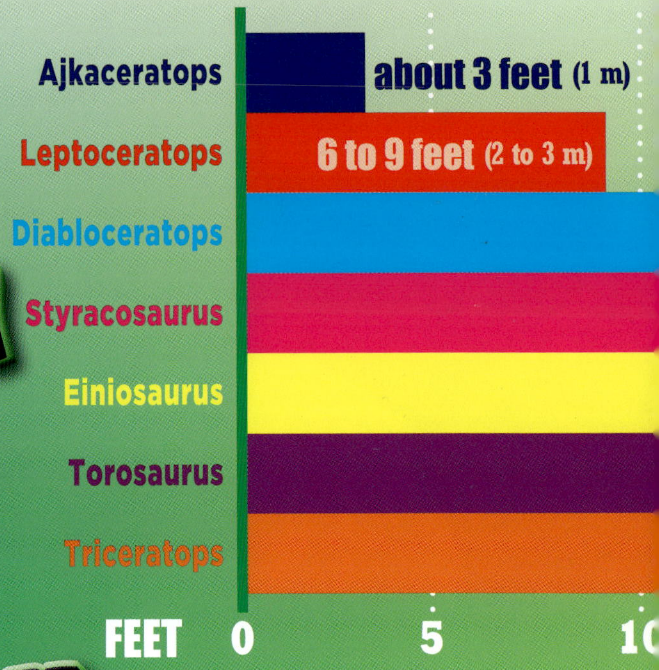

NUMBER OF FACE HORNS

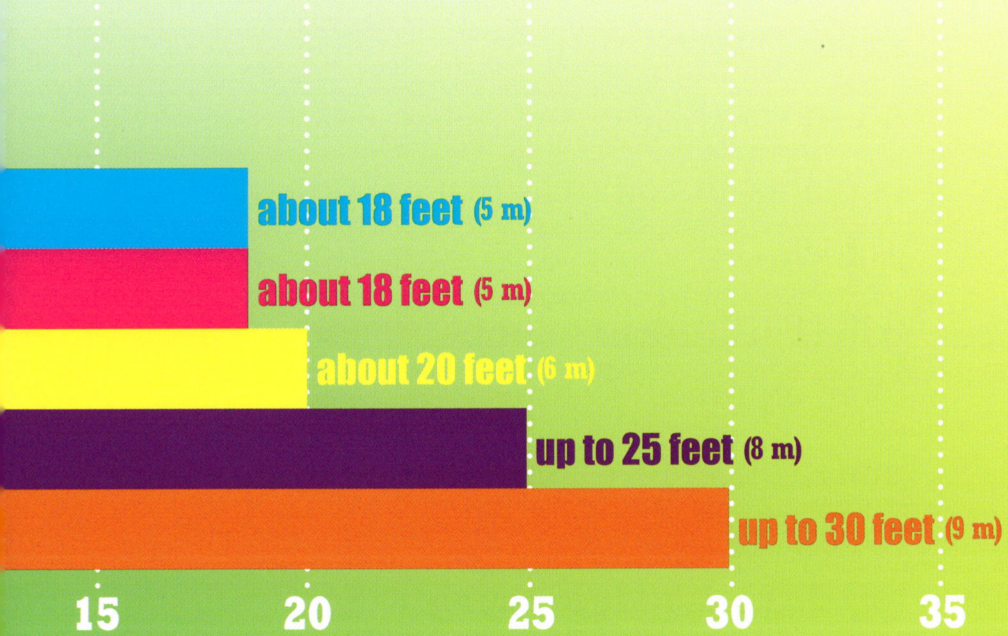

WEIGHT

Torosaurus
up to 18,000 pounds
(8,165 kg)

Triceratops
11,000 to 15,750 pounds
(4,990 to 7,144 kg)

Styracosaurus
6,000 pounds
(2,722 kg)

attract (uh-TRAKT)—to draw someone or something to oneself

fierce (FEERS)—strong or intense

fossil (FAH-sul)—the remains or traces of plants and animals that are preserved as rock

frill (FRIL)—hair or bone around the neck of an animal

mate (MAYT)—to join together to produce young; it's also one of a pair that joins together to produce young.

predator (PRED-uh-tuhr)—an animal that eats other animals

snout (SNOUT)—the projecting part of an animal's face that includes the nose or nose and mouth

survive (sur-VIV)—to remain alive

BOOKS

Peterson, Megan Cooley. *The Dinosaur Extinction: What Really Happened?* History's Mysteries. Mankato, MN: Black Rabbit Books, 2019.

Shofner, Melissa Raé. *Gareth's Guide to Unearthing a Dinosaur.* Gareth Guides to an Extraordinary Life. New York: Gareth Stevens Publishing, 2018.

Waxman, Laura Hamilton. *Discovering Triceratops.* Dinosaurs. Mankato, MN: Amicus, 2019.

WEBSITES

Dinosaurs
discoverymindblown.com/category/dinosaurs/

Horned Dinosaurs
www.kidsdinos.com/horned-dinosaur/

Prehistoric World
www.nationalgeographic.com/science/the-prehistoric-world/

INDEX